THERAPY PROCESSES

1. WHAT HELPS WHEN YOU ARE UPSET?

Objective

Here is an opportunity to explore how responses affect someone who is experiencing strong negative emotion.

Introduction

Therapists often interact with people who are experiencing strong negative emotions, including sadness, anger, and fear. The goal of the interaction may be to experience and express the negative emotion or to calm and soothe it. How the therapist responds to the client's upset can impact the direction the interaction takes and may affect future therapist-client interactions. Sometimes, responses to emotion can have more to do with therapist discomfort than with client goals.

Exploration

1. A friend calls to tell you that his dog was just run over and killed. He has tears in his voice and sounds desperate.

   a) How might you respond to your friend whose dog has died?

   b) Why would you respond that way, that is, what would your goal be and how would your response achieve that goal?

   c) Suppose your dog has just had a litter of puppies. Would you offer one? Why or why not?

2. Think back on a recent time when you were upset.

   a) Describe what you were feeling.

   b) Whom did you seek out to tell about it? Why that person? Whom did you not seek out? Why not those people?

   c) What did that person say that was helpful and what was not? Why and why not? Was how the person said it important?

3. Discuss how strong negative emotions were responded to in your family of origin. How do you feel this has affected the way you respond to upset now?

4. A child comes to her mother sobbing because she has accidentally stepped on a favorite toy that was a gift from her grandmother, breaking it. "What will grandma think?" is all she can say. Her mother says, "Don't cry. It's only a toy. Besides it was an accident."

   a) How do you think the child would react?

b) Make up a different response that you might give. Compare it with the mother's response. How do you think the child's reaction would be different?

5. **Client:** That jerk of a boss! How dare he ask me to stay late on Friday. I'm quitting.

   Therapist 1: Be careful. Jobs are hard to get.

   Therapist 2: I can feel your anger…go on.

   a) Make up client responses to each of the therapist responses.

   b) You be Therapist 3. How might you respond? What might the reaction be?

   c) Analyze the three therapists' responses.

6. **Chris:** Another shooting at the mall…I'm so scared, I'm shaking…we're not safe anywhere…

   a) How might you respond as Chris' parent?

    b) How might you respond as Chris' roommate?

    c) How might you respond as Chris' therapist?

    d) Discuss differences between your responses in a), b), and c). In particular, what does this say about therapists' responses to upset?

7. Discuss what you have learned in this exploration about interactions with individuals who are experiencing strong negative emotions. Take into account such considerations as goals, different emotions, different relationships, and what gets in the way of helpful responding.

8. Give some thought to upset that might come up in therapy. Based on that, role-play situations with a colleague in which each of you responds to strong negative emotions of the other. Discuss the responses.

9. Engage in a group discussion concerning what helps when a person is upset. Share your reactions to this exploration, particularly any surprises or revelations.

2. WHAT ABOUT ADVICE?

Objective

You will have an opportunity to explore the role of advice in the change processes in our lives and particularly in therapy.

Introduction

If advice were the sure cure, we would all be fixed since it is readily available. Sometimes, being told what to do is just what we need. Often, however, even if advice is good, we are not ready to heed it. Here you will explore when advice is and is not helpful.

Exploration

1. **Client:** I just don't know what to do. My grades are a mess!

    Therapists 1: How about some studying?

    Therapists 2: You really sound discouraged.

    Therapists 3: Tell me more about it.

    Discuss how each response might impact the client and where the conversation might lead.

2. *Client:* I'm not getting any better. Do you think I should be evaluated for medication?

   Therapists 1: Makes sense to me.

   Therapists 2: Tell me more…

   Therapists 3: I don't think you need meds. Have you been doing the homework we agreed on?

   Discuss how each response might impact the client and where the conversation might lead.

3. Tom wakes up hung over and says to his roommate, "I feel just awful. I think I'll cut class."

   a) What might you say if you were Tom's roommate? How might your response impact Tom?

   b) How might your response differ if you were Tom's therapist?

4. A college student asks her academic adviser, "If I'm going to be a premed major, what courses should I take first?"

   a) What would be the most helpful response? Why?

b) In what ways does this situation differ from that in 3?

5. Student therapist to supervisor: "I'm just lost. I don't know how to help this client."

a) If you were the supervisor, how might you respond to the student?

b) Now put yourself in the student's shoes. What would your response to the supervisor be?

6. a) How do your parents handle advice giving and how do you respond?

b) Do your parents handle advice differently now than they did when you were younger?

c) How has your parents' advice-giving pattern affected yours?

    d) What have been the other important influences on your advice-giving style?

7. a) Describe recent instances in your life when advice you received was helpful and when it was not.

    b) What made some advice helpful and other advice not?

8. a) Now, describe instances when you have given advice that was helpful and instances when advice given was not helpful.

    b) What made some advice you gave helpful and other advice not helpful? How could you tell if your advice was helpful?

9. Do you ever respond to advice with, "But you just don't understand?" If so, give an instance. What could the advice giver have done to help you feel understood?

10. Discuss the role of each of the following in determining the effectiveness of advice:

    a) The relationship between the giver and the receiver.

    b) The frame of mind of the receiver.

    c) What interaction preceded the advice.

    d) Whether or not the advice was sought.

    e) The type of problem the advice is addressing.

    f) The congruence of the advice to the receiver's view of things.

g) How it is presented.

11. Discuss any potential impact of advice given on the nature of the relationship between the giver and receiver in terms of equality.

12. There are those who feel that an experienced therapist often knows what a client should do and should tell the client. Others feel that knowledge is so personal that advice giving is often presumptuous, disrespectful, and harmful. What is your view of the role of advice in therapy?

13. Engage in a group discussion on the role of advice in therapy, including:

- When it is helpful.

- When you know what is right for a person.

- What impact advice giving has on a relationship.

- How therapy is different from other settings regarding advice.

3. GOALS

Objective

Here you have an opportunity to explore the function of goals in our lives.

Introduction

At one extreme, a goal can be a slave driver, providing the content for self-abuse if the goal is not perfectly achieved. At the other extreme, the absence of goals can result in directionless behavior that does not accumulate gains or provide satisfaction. Between these extremes, goals can provide a sense of direction in making choices, setting priorities, and investing energies.

Exploration

1. List the goals in your life.

2. Choose a goal, past or present, the pursuit of which brings you pleasure and satisfaction. Discuss how this goal affected/affects your life.

3. Choose a goal, past or present, that is less satisfying to you. Discuss how this goal affected/affects your life.

4. How might you adjust your less satisfying goals or use them differently to make them work better for you?

5. a) Discuss the nature of any difference between short-term and long-range goals.

   b) How can distinguishing between short-term and long-range goals be useful to you?

6. Reflect on those people who have influenced the goals in your life.

   a) What roles have your parents played in the formation of your goals? How do you wish they had handled goals differently with you?

   b) What roles have others played in your goal formation?

7. *Client:* I'm 34 now and I had wanted to be a vice president of my company by the time I'm 35. All this hard work and good performance stuff is no good. It is going to take too long.

   a) Discuss how this person's goal seems to be affecting her.

b) How might you intervene as this person's therapist?

8. *Client:* I don't want anything. I live from day to day and feel aimless.

   a) Discuss how this person's approach to goals may be affecting him.

   b) How might a person get into that situation?

   c) How might you intervene as this person's therapist?

9. *Therapist:* Progress toward many goals is more like sailing than motor
   boating. A sailboat has to change directions in response to prevailing winds
   and often cannot sail directly toward the destination. A motorboat can head
   straight for the destination goal.

   a) Discuss the message this analogy might convey.

   b) Draw a picture representing the analogy.

c) Make up a client situation that the analogy might fit.

d) How might you respond to a client who says, "When I go sailing, I just like to sail around without a destination"?

10. **Client:** I hate college. I really love working with electricity, but my parents just will not hear of my becoming an electrician. I don't know what to do.

a) Discuss the client's problem in terms of goals.

b) What approach might therapy with this client take?

11. Champions and others who achieve great recognition often describe a relentless, maybe driven, pursuit of a goal. On the other hand, goals can be seen as reducing the enjoyment of the moment. In light of this observation and the rest of this exploration, where do you feel goals should fit into people's lives?

12. Engage in a group discussion about the role of goals in life and how that impinges on therapy. Address how goals are formed, how they can impact life, and how they can change.

4. ANALOGIES

Objective

A wide repertoire of communication skills is important for a therapist. In this exploration you will gain experience with the use of analogy in communication.

Introduction

A businessman who was experiencing a frightening upheaval in his personal life was embarrassed, overwhelmed, and feeling that things were hopeless. His therapist said, "It's kind of like a company that has been selling a product for years. When sales declined, management didn't know what to do. Consultants were brought in. Changes were made. New and better products emerged and profits soared. The whole process was the occasion for much disruption and anxiety throughout the company. But, great improvements resulted. Such changes are sometimes needed, aren't they?"

The analogy enabled the businessman to step back a little and see what he was experiencing as more respectable. It also brought to his mind many problem-solving techniques that were familiar to him in a work setting, but which he had not considered applicable to his personal life. Since he was very upset, there was some risk that the businessman might feel that the analogy trivialized the problems he was experiencing.

Exploration

1. Describe your understanding of what an analogy is.

2. What could the therapist in the Introduction do to minimize the possibility that the businessman would feel trivialized by the analogy?

3. List other (than those given in the introduction) potential values and risks of the analogy given.

4. What would you say if you were the therapist and the businessman said, "I don't get it. What does a company have to do with my problems?"

5. To the anxious parent of a learning disabled child, a therapist might say, "Elementary school is a pretty narrow road, and a lot of kids slip onto the shoulder and need help staying on the road. The road gets wider in high school, wider yet in college, and is dramatically wider after school where people can be successful with a wide range of strengths and weaknesses."

   a) What message do you get from the analogy?

   b) What impact might the analogy have on the parent?

   c) Analyze the analogy, noting its strengths and weaknesses, and make any changes that you feel would improve it.

6. Suppose you had a client who tended to give up quickly on goals that were not immediately attainable and who was frustrated by the resulting aimlessness of her life. Use the analogy of a tacking sailboat and its progress toward a goal to make a point. (Tacks are directional adjustments a sailboat has to make to take advantage of the wind. Most tacks are not directly toward the destination, but have the boat making progress in that general direction. This contrasts with a powerboat that can motor directly towards its destination.)

7. Live, supple tree limbs are easier to bend, but harder to break than dry, rigid ones. Describe a client situation where this might provide a useful analogy and describe how the analogy might help.

8. A golfer with a putt to win the championship and a basketball player with a free throw to win the game are both in situations where they need to concentrate on the act, putting or shooting, rather than on the outcome, winning or losing. Describe a client situation where you might use one of these as an analogy and describe how the analogy might help.

9. To build up your biceps at the gym requires repeated effort over time with little apparent day-to-day improvement. Describe a client situation where this might provide a useful analogy and describe how it might help.

10. Describe a client and the client's problem. Then create an analogy that the client might relate to and that addresses the client's problem. How might the analogy help?

11. What analogies have you found useful in your life…for yourself or in your work with others?

12. Describe your sense of the usefulness and limitations of analogies as a tool in communication.

13. Engage in a group discussion on the use of analogies. You may want to share your favorite ones…ones that flopped, too.

5. CONFRONTATION

Objective

Here you will have an opportunity to explore effective confrontation and its therapeutic use.

Introduction

Confrontation is one of the basic tasks of therapy. While the word, "confrontation," can have a negative connotation, the therapeutic use of confrontation has the positive goal of bringing the client face to face with useful information. This goal requires that the confrontation be understood, tolerated, and accepted. Everyday phrases that relate to confrontation include "give direct feedback" and "point out."

Exploration

1. Tom has been drinking, and his date, Sally, is worried about him driving...

   Sally 1: Tom, you've had too much to drink, so why don't you let me drive?

   Sally 2: Tom, why don't you let me drive home?

   Sally 3: Tom, do you remember when we talked about telling each other when it was not a good time to drive? I think now is one of those times.

   Sally 4: Tom, if you are going to drive, I'm going home with Jane.

   Discuss Sally's responses with an eye toward their being understood, tolerated, and accepted.

2. Discuss your understanding of the meaning of confrontation. Give some related words and phrases.

3. Reflect on a time when you were confronted about a difficult or sensitive topic.

    a) How were you confronted and by whom?

    b) How did you react to the confrontation?

    c) How might the confrontation have been presented more effectively?

4. Now reflect on a situation where you confronted someone.

    a) How did you do it?

    b) How did it work?

    c) How would you do it again?

5. How were confrontations handled in your family as you were growing up? Reflect on any connections between this and your style of confrontation.

6. Think about an acquaintance who tends to do something that you feel is self-defeating. Describe two ways you could confront your friend. Which might work best? Why?

7. ***Client:*** I fell asleep at my desk again. I'm going to get into big trouble at work.

   Therapist 1: Do you have any sense of why you're so tired?

   Therapist 2: Did you watch the late show again?

   Therapist 3: Last time you fell asleep, you said the late show was the villain...

   Discuss each response and its likely impact. Make another response.

8. A new client comes to a therapist's office in a revealing dress.

   Therapist 1: (After about 15 minutes) Would you share with me your intention in wearing that dress?

   Therapist 2: (No mention of dress.)

   Therapist 3: Wow, that's quite a dress you've got on!

Again, discuss each response. How might the impact have been different if therapy had been going on for months? Create another response.

9. *Teenage Client:* My parents got all over me for bringing the car home on empty!

Therapist 1: How did you react?

Therapist 2: Parents will do that, won't they?

Therapist 3: I guess it does seem right to return it the way you found it.

Discuss each therapist response and its likely impact. Create another response.

10. Discuss any generalization you have observed about confrontations concerning, for example, goals, timing, by whom, wording, and connection to what is already accepted.

11. Choose a partner, make up scenarios and practice confrontations.

12. Engage in a group discussion on confrontations. Be sure to include considerations like those in 10 above.

6. EMPATHY

Objective

Here you can explore the nature of empathy and its role in your life, therapy, and human interactions in general.

Introduction

Empathy has to do with seeing the world through another person's eyes and understanding it from his or her perspective...getting into that person's reality while maintaining a sense of your own. Genuinely communicated empathy can make an important contribution to the therapy process. We differ in our goals, skills, and willingness regarding empathy, and we tend to be empathic in some circumstances and not in others.

Exploration

1. What does the word "empathy" mean to you?

2. Describe a person in your life whom you have experienced as empathic with you. How does this affect your relationship with this person?

3. Give an example of an empathic encounter in your life. How did the encounter affect you?

4. How could empathy have an undesirable impact? Give an example.

5. How did empathy enter the interactions in your family when you were a child?

6. Sam's roommate, John, has a straight-A average. John comes back from a test near tears saying, "I blew it. I got a C at best. There goes my straight-A average." Discuss each of the following responses by Sam from the standpoint of empathy and its impact on John.

    a) "No sweat, John, you'll do better than you think."

    b) "Boy, I wish I had your grade problems."

    c) "I'm really sorry, John. What are you going to do?"

    d) "That's tough. I know your good grades mean a lot to you."

    e) Give an empathic response of your own. What would it feel like for you to say this?

7. a) Make up an example like number 6.

    b) Give an empathic and nonempathic response.

    c) What makes one empathic and the other not?

d) Which kind of response are you more likely to give?

8. A client says, "I'm so angry at my husband...all he lives for is to spend the weekend hunting."

   a) Give what you feel might be an empathic response.

   b) Give what you guess would be an unempathic response.

   c) Discuss the difference between your responses in a) and b).

9. An eight-year-old child comes home from school sniffling. His mother says, "What's wrong, dear." The child says, "Nothing," and slouches off to his room.

   a) Give what you feel would be an empathic response.

   b) Give what you feel would be an unempathic response.

   c) Again, discuss the difference.

10. What do you see as the role of empathy in therapy?

11. Make up therapeutic situations where the communication of empathy might be:

    a) Ineffective

    b) Harmful

12. Summarize what you have learned about empathy in this exploration.

13. Engage in a group discussion on empathy. Be sure to address:

    • What empathy is.

    • The impact of empathy on human behavior.

    • The role of empathy in therapy.

    • Can empathy hurt?

7. JUDGMENTS

Objective

Here you can explore the role of judgments in your life and in the therapeutic process.

Introduction

Judgments are conclusions we reach after looking at something from our own point of view. Judgments can help us make decisions that are consistent with our goals and well-being. Everyday judgments include, whether to turn right or left, whether it is safe to lend him my car or not, and whether to avoid dessert after dinner or splurge. Career, job, and life-partner choices involve weighty judgments with long-term consequences. As a therapist, you make judgments such as diagnosis, treatment plan, and when and how to intervene. You will also be a party to the judgment making of your clients.

Many times, clients' judgments will jibe with yours. Oftentimes clients' judgments will differ from your own as they view things from their own perspective. Sometimes they will judge things very differently than you would. Sometimes their judgments may not work for them, which may be part of the reason they seek treatment.

Exploration

1. A college junior comes to her therapist and says: "I have straight-A's in computer science, and I've been offered a job by a small, new computer firm that has a software idea they think will go big. I'm tempted to quit school and go with them. What do you think?"

   Therapist 1: You only have one more year of school. Why risk your degree on a long shot?

   Therapist 2: Why not go for it? You're young and some of those software companies get bought up, and...

   Therapist 3: You sound excited. Tell me more.

   a) In your judgment, what would be best for the student to do?

b) Analyze each of the three therapist responses as to appropriateness and impact.

c) How might you respond, and where would you want your response to lead the interaction? Describe any misgivings you might have.

2. Suppose a client came to you and said: "I have two children. I work. My husband works, and we just make ends meet. My husband puts me down all of the time. He drinks too much, and I don't really love him any more..."

a) What do you think the woman should do? What might happen if she did that?

b) Where might you want your conversation to go with her? What might you say to her?

3. Suppose a client comes to a session drunk.

    a) What might your reaction be?

    b) What might you want to accomplish in your intervention with this client?

    c) What might you say to the client?

4. Think of recent situations in your life in which someone told you his or her judgment of what you ought to do.

    a) Describe the situations and your reactions.

    b) When was it helpful to be told, when not, and why?

5. Think of recent situations when you discussed a problem with someone who did not offer an opinion of what you ought to do.

   a) Describe the situations and your reactions.

   b) Analyze how helpful the discussions were and why.

6. *Client:* I stayed up all night studying and got an A!

   Evaluate the following therapist responses.

   a) "That's great!"

   b) "What did that do to your performance at work today?"

   c) "How did that work for you?"

d) "It sounds like you haven't been studying between tests."

7. Have you ever been given someone's opinion and responded, "Yes but you don't understand"?

    a) What does this say about your internal response to what the person said?

    b) What might a person do to maximize your receptivity to his or her response?

8. If the therapist's goal is to help clients make judgments that serve their goals, describe any possible hazard in such therapist responses as "that's great," "good job," "nice going."

9. a) What does the word "judgmental" mean to you?

    b) Do you consider yourself to be judgmental? Why do you think that?

c) What/who has most strongly influenced your style of handling judgments?

10. a) What judgments must a therapist make?

   b) What judgments should a therapist seldom articulate? Why?

   c) What judgments might it be good for a therapist to articulate occasionally?

11. Summarize what you have learned here about judgments and their role in therapy.

12. Engage in a group discussion on judgments and their role in therapy. Be aware of each other's reactions to judgments being articulated.

8. EXPANDING OPTIONS

Objective

Here you can learn to view certain situations from a broader perspective, which can be helpful in dealing with them.

Introduction

Sometimes it is useful to think of things as either black or white, yes or no, do or don't, x or y. Many times, though, it helps to add alternatives. The alternatives are useful because many real situations are too complicated to be treated as either black or white. For example:

> *Joe:* If you loved me, you'd go to the game with me.

> *Jane:* It's not that, it's...

> *Joe:* That's it. I've had it!

Maybe Jane does not love Joe and that is the reason why she does not want to go to the game. But, there are other possibilities. For example, she may be very uncomfortable in large crowds; she may be put off by Joe's ultimatum; she may still be angry because Joe would not go somewhere with her yesterday; she may be turned off by the game; she may be worn out from a tough week and be longing for a nap...

Joe did not have to box himself into this "either/or" situation: either you go to the game <u>or</u> you do not love me. He could have viewed this as an "and/or" situation: maybe she does not love me, "and/or" maybe it is something about the game, "and/or" maybe it is something between us, "and/or" maybe it's something going on in her life... There can be many reasons why Joe boxed himself in: maybe he has a habit of viewing things narrowly, "and/or" maybe he is afraid that if he believes in Jane's love, he'll be disappointed, "and/or" maybe he is trying to shame Jane into going to the game...

Clients often come into therapy having boxed themselves in with such "either/or" thinking. It is often important for the therapist not to get into the same box and to be able to introduce some "and/or" thinking.

Exploration

1. Suppose that Joe and Jane had their exchange in a therapy session. Consider these therapist responses:

Therapist 1: Joe, I hear that you are feeling unloved. Before you leave, would you be willing to listen to the rest of what Jane has to say?

Therapist 2: Joe you are not considering the options. You're saying, either she goes to the game or she does not love you.

Therapist 3: Joe, it sounds like your feelings are hurt, say some more.

a) Discuss the three responses and what the impact of each might be.

b) In light of your discussion in a), how might you validate Joe's feelings and, at the same time, open him up to alternative ways of viewing Jane's behavior?

2. *Client:* I used to really like being with him, but he forgot our lunch yesterday. I'm through.

Therapist 1: I can see you're really bummed about his forgetting...

Therapist 2: I hear you enjoy being with him and are hurt by his forgetting.

Therapist 3: Have you considered a way to address your hurt and keep him as a friend?

a) Express the client's situation as an "either/or" box.

b) Expand the options available to the client by phrasing some possibilities in terms of "and/ors."

c) Analyze the potential impact of the three therapist responses.

d) Propose a response you might give as a therapist.

3. *Client:* I can't get into the section of organic chemistry I need. I might as well quit.

a) Phrase the client's view as an "either/or" statement.

b) Broaden the situation with some "and/or" possibilities.

    c) What might your response be as therapist?

4. ***Client:*** I used to think that she was such a neat woman. Then, I learned she voted for Jones in the last election. How can I spend time with someone who voted for Jones?

    a) Phrase this as an "either/or" box.

    b) Open the box with some "and/or" possibilities.

    c) How might you respond as therapist to help the client open the box?

5. Think of a situation in your life where you are boxed in by "either/or" thinking.

    a) Phrase the situation as an "either/or" box.

    b) Expand the situation by giving "and/or" possibilities.

c) Why did you box yourself in?

6. Think of a situation where a friend is boxed in by "either/or" thinking.

a) Describe the situation as an "either/or" box.

b) Open the box with some "and/ors."

c) What might be keeping the friend in a box?

d) How might you help the friend out of the box? How might your approach be different if you were your friend's therapist and not a friend?

7. a) Describe some situations that are usefully thought of as "either/or" boxes.

   b) What is it about those situations that is different?

8. Summarize what you have learned in this exploration about expanding options. Do you have any reactions?

9. Engage in a group discussion about "either/or" boxes, why we get into them, and what helps us get out of them.

9. GETTING THE REAL MESSAGE

Objective

Here you can explore listening for and responding to what may be underlying what people say and do.

Introduction

Things are not always as they seem when it comes our feelings. We say we hate someone we love. We act angry when we are scared or hurt. We distance ourselves from someone we want to be close to. We shed tears of joy. In such situations, we are not usually intentionally misrepresenting. The feelings that lie behind our behavior can be out of our awareness. Often this lack of awareness has a self-protective function of avoiding vulnerability and pain. Sometimes, however, there can be a significant personal price for this protection. For example:

Tamara: I was downtown with Toni. It's special when we get together. We were getting ready for lunch when we ran into Jane. She and Toni were talking like old friends and ignored me. I was just furious at Toni and left as soon as I could.

In this example Tamara is aware of her anger. She may well not be aware of other feelings that underlie the anger. This lack of awareness may seriously affect how Tamara handles the situation with Toni.

A response to Tamara could focus on the **content** of the situation, it could address the **apparent feelings**, or it could address the **underlying feelings**.

Exploration

1. a) If you were Tamara's therapist, how might you respond to her?

b) *Therapist 1:* Are you sure Toni meant to ignore you?

Therapist 2: I hear that you are really angry at Toni.

Therapist 3: I think I hear some hurt feelings under your anger. Indicate which therapist response addresses content, which addresses apparent feelings, and which underlying feelings. Discuss where each of these responses might lead.

2. *Client:* I studied as hard as I could and I failed the exam...lousy course.

a) Give three therapist responses.

b) Discuss your therapist responses. Indicate whether they address the content, apparent feelings, or underlying feelings.

c) Where would the response, "Tell me more about how you feel about the course," fit in?

3. *Client:* Joe has been sucking up to the boss and taking credit for everything I'm doing. Today, Joe got caught in a serious error of his own. It was a blast to watch the boss chew him out!

    a) Give at least three therapist responses.

    b) Discuss each response in terms of what it addresses and where it might lead.

4. In response to a therapist question, a client says, "I won't tell you. It's none of your business."

    a) Give at least three therapist responses.

    b) Discuss the therapist responses in terms of where they were directed and where they might lead.

c) How might you feel if a client said that to you? How might your feelings affect your response? Would you be most likely to respond to the client's content, apparent feelings, or underlying feelings?

5. *Client:* Who do they think they are? They're bringing in new computers, demanding that us old-timers use them, and hiring young people who already know how to use them. A bunch of hot shots!

a) Give at least three therapist responses.

b) Discuss where the session might go with each response.

c) How might the client's job situation be affected by where the session goes?

d) How might the therapist's personal reaction to what the client said affect her response?

6. a) Create a client scenario with three therapist responses addressing content, apparent feelings, and underlying feelings.

   b) Analyze each therapist response in terms of what it addresses and the direction the interaction might take.

7. *Client:* I came home last night and found my dog dead. I spent the whole evening burying him.

   Therapist 1: Tell me what you did.

   Therapist 2: What were you feeling while you did that?

   a) Discuss these two responses in terms of what they address and where they might lead.

b) Why might a therapist give each response? Might the reasons have anything to do with the therapist's personal response to the client's loss?

8. a) Describe a situation in your own life when the apparent feelings you expressed were different than the underlying feelings.

b) Were you aware of the discrepancy at that time? If not, when and how did you become aware?

9. Summarize your experience in this exploration, being sure to address different therapist responses, reasons for them, the impact of therapist personal reactions, and different outcomes for the client.

10. Engage in a group discussion related to underlying messages, the value and difficulty of pursuing them, and what was learned in doing this exploration.

10. HUMAN CHANGE

Objective

Here is an opportunity to explore different kinds of human change and their relative difficulty.

Introduction

The goal of therapy is change. Clients as well as their therapists can become frustrated at the slow pace of certain kinds of change, particularly when the change seems clearly in the best interest of the client. Some human change can be easy and quick; other change can require a lengthy struggle. One reason for the difference is the different human systems involved in the changes. For example, changes in emotion, habit, knowledge, point of view, skill, and values can proceed at quite different paces.

Emotions involve parts of the brain (the "old brain") that are shared with other animals. As you know, changes in animal behavior often require training that takes time. It is not surprising that emotional functioning can change slowly.

Habits and skills can affect many different human systems and can differ widely in their resistance to change.

Knowledge involves the neocortex that is uniquely human, very adaptable, and can change quickly. New information can be learned with relative ease and speed. Knowledge learning can be impeded, for example, by its conflict with values, which involve emotions.

Point of view and values tend to affect how we process all of the information we receive and how we respond. Consequently, a change in values or point of view affects all of our functioning in all aspects of our life, in ways that are often difficult to predict. It is not surprising that changes with such far-reaching consequences would be approached cautiously and slowly, even if the change appears to be very desirable.

Exploration

1. Think about a personal change you struggle with and discuss how your struggle makes sense in light of differing difficulties of changes described in the introduction.

2. Think about a personal change you have made with relative ease and discuss how the ease of this change makes sense in light of the introduction.

3. For each domain listed below, identify a change you would like to make, how you might go about making the change, and how easy you feel the change would be for you.

   a) Emotion

   b) Habit

c) Knowledge

d) Point of view

e) Skill

f) Values

4. Suppose you have a client who as a child internalized the message that he is a bad person. Suppose further that the client persists self-destructively with that message despite considerable data to the contrary. Discuss reasons why this seemingly useless belief might be resistant to change.

5. A client is highly reactive, gets upset at small things, and has trouble getting back on track. Discuss the possible nature and difficulty of change for this client.

6. A man was brought up in a home where his mother stayed home, kept house, and took care of the children. His wife was brought up by her single-parent mother who took care of everything and taught her daughter to do the same. The couple are in love, but are struggling with their marriage. What might need to change in order to smooth out their relationship? Discuss what might be involved in the change process.

7. A bright college freshman is having difficulty adjusting to the demands of time allocation and money management. Discuss the possible changes that might be needed to be made by this person.

8. A chef who works late at a busy restaurant "calms" down after work with a six-pack of beer. His physician says he should quit. What problems do you expect he will run into in the change process?

9. A client is terrified of flying and will only travel on the ground. What do you think would be involved in getting the client airborne?

10. Which of the domains of change (emotion, habit, etc.) do you think change most like the way muscles strengthen, that is, as the result of repeated, challenging effort? Discuss.

11. Discuss how client motivation to change might vary from client to client and how it might affect the change process.

12. How might you as therapist respond to the following?

    Client: I'm sick and tired of this. I've seen you six times now, and I still have trouble opening my mouth in class.

13. Summarize what you have learned about human change in this exploration.

14. Engage in a group discussion about human change. Be sure to discuss your personal experience of change and any implications for the therapy process.

11. PROCESS/CONTENT INTERVENTIONS

Objective

You will have an opportunity to explore process interventions, to distinguish them from content interventions, and to explore the use of each in therapy.

Introduction

Often it is our pattern of thought or action that gets us into trouble, not any particular thought or action. When a therapist addresses a pattern of behavior, it is called a process intervention. For example,

> **Client:** Mom pestered me about my room. I got angry, skipped school, and ended up in big trouble.
>
> **Therapist 1:** Your mom really angers you...
>
> **Therapist 2:** Your anger gets you in trouble doesn't it?

Therapist 1's intervention focuses on the client's feelings, which is often a good thing to do. However, Therapist 2 addresses what may be a *pattern* of responding self-destructively to anger. This pattern may be related to why the client came into therapy, and such process interventions may help the client become aware of the pattern so that it can be modified.

Often, the client is focused on the content of his problem. For example, on how dirty his room is, on the fact that it's his room and not his mother's, or on the idea that no one has the right to tell him what to do. It can be enticing for the therapist to get caught up in the content along with the client. However, if the therapist can step back, focus on the problematic process, and bring it to the client's awareness, this method can facilitate change. Sometimes, when the client is focused on the content, it must be addressed by the therapist before any process intervention can be heard by the client.

Exploration

1. **Client:** Susan told me to get lost, and I went out and got drunk.

    Therapist 1: Susan's been giving you a hard time.

    Therapist 2: Sounds like one of your flights from pain. Doesn't it?

a) Discuss the two interventions and their possible impact on the client.

b) *Therapist 3:* Sounds like a rough night…(later)…Is this one of those situations where avoiding one pain creates another?

Discuss when you might use this intervention instead of Therapist 2's.

2. Consider the following interaction from a couple's therapy session.

Husband: You really enjoyed lunch today.

Wife: You zeroed in a little on the waitress yourself.

Therapist 1: Tell me more about what happened.

Therapist 2: You guys really keep the needle in each other.

Discuss the two therapist interventions and their likely impact on the clients.

3. Two friends, Tom and Jim, are talking…

Tom: Jim, get off my back. It's none of your business.

Jim 1: What do you mean it's none of my business? Last week…

Jim 2: What's going on? That's the third time you've jumped on me this week.

Discuss the difference between Jim's two responses and where each might lead the conversation.

4. People tend to address content more than process in their personal conversations. Discuss why this might be.

5. Discuss a situation in your life where a process response might be more effective than the way you have been responding.

6. *Client:* I'm short on money. I was up all night studying for school and had to call in sick at work.

   a) Give a process intervention.

   b) Give a content intervention.

7. *Wife:* I would like to spend more time with you on weekends.

   Husband: Yeah? Last week I was home Saturday. Where were you?

   a) Give a content intervention as the couple's therapist.

   b) Give a process intervention.

   c) How might the nature and quality of your relationship with the couple affect your choice of intervention and the impact of your intervention?

8. Make up a client statement and two therapist responses, one a process intervention and one a content intervention.

Client:

Therapist 1:

Therapist 2:

9. Describe in your own words:

   a) What a process intervention is and contrast it to a content intervention.

   b) Those therapy situations that you feel might call for process interventions.

10. Have a conversation with a colleague. Note any process comments and their impact.

11. Engage in a group discussion about process interventions and when they could be useful in therapy and elsewhere. Look for opportunities to comment on the process of formulating and discussing ideals in your discussion group.

12. QUESTIONS

Objective

Here you have an opportunity to explore the impact on therapy of different forms of questions.

Introduction

How you word the questions you ask will affect the kind of answers you get. It will also affect the impact of the questions on the answerer.

For example, "why" questions will tend to evoke reasoning and explanation. The questioner has to be careful because some people hear certain "why" questions as criticisms to which they may respond defensively, trying to make sense out of what they did.

"What" questions may tend to evoke description. On the other hand, "how" questions may help individuals focus on the process of their life. When asking about feelings, "how" questions can evoke one-word judgments. For example, compare the following "feeling" questions:

Type of Question	Question	Possible Response
How Question	How are you feeling?	OK.
What Question	What are you feeling?	Pretty sad.
Why Question	Why are you feeling sad?	My dog died.

Sometimes, "Tell me more" can get the job done in a less directive way than asking an explicit question.

Exploration

1. *Client:* Last night was terrible. My girlfriend broke up with me and then I got drunk.

   Therapist 1: Why did you do that?

   Therapist 2: What happened?

   Therapist 3: Why was it terrible?

   Therapist 4: How did you feel?

   a) How do you think the client would respond to Therapist 1?

   b) How do you think the client would respond to Therapist 2?

   c) How do you think the client would respond to Therapist 3?

   d) How do you think the client would respond to Therapist 4?

2. ***Client:*** After three years of avoiding him, I called him last night.

   Therapist 1: What happened?

   Therapist 2: What was that like for you?

   Discuss where each of the therapist "what" questions might lead.

3. Make up a client statement and "what" and "why" therapist questions. Then explore the different client responses you would expect.

4. ***Client:*** I almost binged on a bag of cookies last night, but I didn't!

   Therapist 1: How did you do that?

   Therapist 2: What are your thoughts about that?

   Discuss where each therapist question might lead.

5. Make up a client statement and "how" and "what" therapist questions. Then explore the different client responses you would expect.

6. Client walks in and plops down.

    Therapist 1: How are you feeling?

    Therapist 2: What are you feeling?

    Discuss possible client answers.

7. Make up a client statement and two therapist questions related to feelings. Then discuss where each question may lead the conversation.

8. *Client:* It's been quite a day!

    Therapist 1: Tell me more.

    Therapist 2: What happened?

    Discuss the impact of the therapists' responses.

9. Make up a client statement and two therapist responses, one a question and one a "tell me more" response. Then discuss the impacts of the therapists' responses.

10. a) If a client is doing something and appears to be denying its consequences, what kind of questions might you emphasize? Why?

    b) If a client is doing something that is contrary to his or her stated beliefs, what kind of questions might you emphasize? Why?

    c) Discuss the use of "tell me more" and when you might emphasize it.

    d) If a client is very sensitive to criticism, what kind of questions might you emphasize and why?

11. Pair up with a colleague and have a conversation in which you pay particular attention to the questions you ask each other.

    a) What did you observe about questions and answers?

    b) Were there differences in questioning style between the two of you? How do you explain any differences?

12. Summarize your thoughts about questions in terms of the responses and internal processes evoked in the responder.

13. Engage in a group discussion on the form of questions and its relationship to the goals and processes of therapy. Give specific examples.

13. TEACHING

Objective

You will have an opportunity to explore how teaching can be used as an analogy for understanding the change process in psychotherapy.

Introduction

Therapy is an interaction intended to promote human change. Teaching is another change-focused interaction with which most adults have considerable experience, at least as students.

Some time-honored maxims of teaching include:

- Clarify the goals.

- Start where the student is and lead him or her to the goal.

- Keep track of whether the student is coming along.

- Be attuned to how each student learns best.

- Challenge the student.

- Whenever possible, teach the student to fish rather than giving the student a fish.

The last maxim refers to the old saying that giving someone a fish feeds the person for a day; teaching someone to fish feeds the person for life.

Exploration

1. Do you have anything to add to the list of teaching maxims?

2. Think of a teacher you learned a lot from.

   a) Discuss how this person's teaching meshed with the above maxims.

   b) What do you feel contributed the most to your learning?

3. Discuss the process of appropriate <u>goal clarifying</u> in therapy. How does it differ from the typical teaching situation?

4. *Client:* I really want to get things going with my career, and I want you to help me.

   Discuss how you might follow the teaching maxim of <u>starting where the student is and leading him or her to the goal</u> with this client.

5. How would you <u>keep track of whether the student is coming along</u> with a client in therapy?

6. Discuss the range of ways you can help a client change and how to choose among them as you <u>stay attuned to how each student learns best</u>.

7. Should a therapist <u>challenge</u> a client? If so, how?

8. a) Discuss the meaning of <u>teach the student to fish rather than give the student a fish</u>.

   b) How could that maxim apply to therapy?

9. ***Client:*** This is the third bad relationship I've had this year. Should I call him or not?

   a) Create a therapist response consistent with teaching this client to fish.

   b) Create a therapist response that would be more like giving the client a fish.

10. Discuss to what extent you feel therapy can be thought of as teaching. How does the analogy fit and how does it not?

11. Discuss with your colleagues the extent to which therapy can be considered analogous to teaching and any concepts from teaching that are useful to the therapist. Be sure to address the maxims.

14. TRACKING FEELINGS

Objective

You will have an opportunity to explore the techniques and consequences of paying close attention to the feeling expressions of others.

Introduction

Clients often come to therapy because of uncomfortable feelings they are having. If these feelings are explored, they may lead to problem areas that need attention. A way to explore or "track" someone's feelings is to focus on the words he or she says that seem to reflect feelings. Here is an example:

Client: I'm late…it's been a bad day.

Therapist: Bad day?

Client: Yeah. I've felt anxious ever since I got up.

Therapist: You've felt anxious?

Client: Frightened. This economy has me on edge.

Therapist: Sounds like you feel unsafe. Like on the edge of a cliff?

Client: Yeah, about to be pushed over.

Therapist: Feeling the threat of being pushed?

Client: Into nothingness.

Therapist: What would that be like?

Client: Like I didn't exist. It's happened before.

Therapist: You've lost your sense of self before?

Client: When my mom yells at me.

Exploration

1. Read over the client-therapist interaction above.

   a) Where might the conversation have gone if the therapist responded as follows:

   Client: I'm late. It's been a bad day.

   Therapist: That's OK. The traffic is terrible. What should we talk about?

   b) Discuss the circumstances under which you might respond each way.

2. *Client:* I was playing Nintendo with Joe. Dad came in and said to Joe, "Are you beating old slow-hands there?" I wanted to quit...

   Therapist 1: What did you do?

   Therapist 2: Ouch! That hurt.

   a) Create a client response for each of the two therapist responses.

b) Create a third therapist response that addresses the client's anger.

c) When might you use each of the three responses?

3. *Client:* When I heard the siren go by, I felt weird.

   Therapist 1: Talk to me a little more about this weird feeling.

   Therapist 2: What was going through your mind?

   a) Make up client responses for each of the two therapist responses.

   b) Make up a third therapist response.

c) Describe the difference between each of the therapist responses and how they might affect the direction of the conversation.

4. ***Client:*** I was minding my own business, doing my job, when that jerk of a boss starts hassling me.

   a) Make up two reasonable therapist responses, one that tracks feelings, and one that does not.

   b) Make up client responses to each of your therapist responses.

5. "She called me. At first I was delighted. Then I felt like a fool for being so happy."

    a) Make up two reasonable therapist responses, one that tracks feelings and one that does not.

    b) Make up client responses for both of your therapist responses.

6. Make up a client-therapist conversation that illustrates tracking feelings.

7. Role-play as client and therapist with another person.

    a) With one as therapist and one as client, first have a conversation without paying particular attention to feelings. Then have a further conversation tracking feelings. How did the conversations differ?

b) Swap roles and do as in a).

8. Discuss the meaning and utility of tracking feelings. When would you do it, and when would you not do it?

9. Engage in a group discussion about tracking feelings, addressing:

- What tracking feelings means.

- What it accomplishes.

- When to use it.

- What it demands of you.

15. CREATING A SAFE PLACE

Objective

You will have an opportunity to explore what makes it safe for you to be influenced in certain ways by certain people.

Introduction

It seems natural and healthy that we are careful about whom we let influence us in what ways. We accurately sense that others are pursuing their own agendas and may not have our best interests in mind. To some extent we can protect ourselves by discerning if the other person seems safe to let influence us in a particular way. Each of us has our own criteria for safety. Questions we ask might include:

- Does this person care about my well-being?

- Does this person take me and my point of view seriously?

- Is this person capable of helping me in a particular way?

- Do I see how this person's interests are served by helping me in that way?

Notice that we may let different people influence us in different ways. For example, we might feel quite comfortable receiving investment advice from someone with whom we would not share an emotional problem.

Exploration

1. Think of someone you allow to influence you in some way. Visualize being with her or him.

   a) What is it about this person that makes him or her safe to influence you?

b) What influence does this person have on you?

c) What are ways you would not let this person influence you? Why?

2. Think of someone you like, but are less inclined to be influenced by in the same way as the person in 1. Visualize being with this person.

a) What about this person and his or her way of interacting makes the person less safe for that kind of influence?

b) Are there other ways you would allow this person to influence you? If so, why?

3. Reflect on your experience with this workbook.

    a) In what ways have you been influenced? In what ways, not?

    b) What features of the workbook and your exploration format have made it feel safer to be influenced?

    c) What features of the workbook and your exploration format have made it feel less safe to be influenced?

4. Reflect on what seem to be your criteria for someone to be safe to influence you.

    a) In what ways do your criteria depend on the kind of influence?

    b) What are your criteria to be influenced in the personal and intimate areas you might bring to therapy?

5. *Client:* I had one cookie, hated myself, and then ate the whole bag.

   Analyze the possible impact of each therapist response on the client's experience of safety.

   a) *Therapist:* Oh darn!

   b) *Therapist:* What are you feeling about that now?

   c) *Therapist:* That sounds pretty perfectionistic doesn't it?

   d) *Therapist:* If you get tempted again, call me.

6. *Client:* Guess what! I had one cookie last night, stopped myself from eating more, and put the bag away.

   Evaluate any impact each therapist response might have on the client's experience of safety in the therapeutic relationship.

   a) *Therapist:* Wow! That's wonderful. I'm really proud of you.

b) *Therapist:* How did you do that?

c) *Therapist:* It sounds like you are pleased with yourself.

d) *Therapist:* How did you feel after you did that?

e) *Therapist:* OK. Great. Let's look at what you did so we can make this work for you next time.

7. What possible negative impact on the safety of therapy do you see in positive judgments like 6 a) and e)?

8. Discuss any possible negative impact on the safety of therapy each of the following situations might have.

    a) The client's sister is the therapist's best friend.

    b) The client is a coworker of another client of the therapist.

    c) The client owes the therapist $400 and is about to leave on a ski vacation.

    d) The therapist makes it clear what job she thinks the client should take.

    e) The therapist is publicly visible about his political views.

f) The therapist talks about what happens in therapy sessions with other clients (not mentioning names).

g) The therapist is much younger than the client.

9. Discuss how the arrangements of therapy, e.g., confidentiality, limited structured contact, and payment, contribute to the safety of therapy.

10. Reflect on your experience working with clinical supervisors.

a) What supervisor characteristics have led you to feel safe to be influenced in what ways?

b) What characteristics have gotten in the way of influence?

c) How have you integrated your supervisor's characteristics into your own way of creating a safe place for your clients?

11. a) Describe the ingredients of a therapist's interactive style that would contribute to client safety.

b) Which aspects of a safe style do you think will be most difficult for you to effect?

12. Engage in a group discussion on what makes it safe to be influenced in what ways. Pay particular attention to group members' differing criteria for safety in a therapeutic setting.

16. GOOD-BYES

Objective

You are invited to explore the opportunities that good-byes offer, in particular, the good-byes or terminations of therapy.

Introduction

Most of us say many good-byes, to individuals, groups, and experiences. With good-byes can come, for example, the pain of loss, the satisfaction of accomplishment, and the enlightenment of new perspectives. Good-byes can be viewed as the transition from one of life's chapters to the next. Often such thoughts as, "I don't want to cry," "I'll see them again," or "What good will it do?" get in the way of our realizing the potential for closure and gain that good-byes offer.

The word "termination" has come to be used to describe the process of saying good-bye in therapy. Therapy, as a relationship focused on learning and healing, offers the opportunity to learn about saying good-bye. The therapist can guide the termination process, helping the client to reflect on any changes, and express thoughts and feelings about therapy and the therapist.

Exploration

1. Recall a recent period of time you spent with someone. When you said good-bye, what were you thinking and feeling? What did you say? What do you wish you had said? How do you feel now about the good-bye?

2. Think back on saying good-bye to a good friend because one of you was moving. Again, what did you think and feel; what did you say; what do you wish you had said and done differently; and how do you feel about it now?

3. In a way similar to 1 and 2, reflect on the breaking up of an extended love relationship or friendship.

4. Think back on when you first left home to live on your own. In a way similar to 1 and 2, reflect on your good-byes at that time.

5. We have all experienced endings resulting from death, for example, the death of a beloved public figure, friend, or relative. Choose such a death in your life and reflect on how you said good-bye. What were you thinking and feeling; what did you say and do; what would you have done differently; and how do you feel about the way you said good-bye?

6. Look back over your answers to 1 through 5.

   a) Describe any patterns you see in your good-byes.

   b) Describe any changes you would consider making in the way you say good-bye.

   c) What, if anything, gets in the way of your saying good-bye the way you would like to?

7. Reflect on how good-byes are handled in your family of origin. Indicate any ways you think this might have affected your good-byes.

8. Chris and Pat are college seniors who have shared an apartment for two years. They have generally gotten along, with only occasional spats. Describe what their good-bye process might look like.

9. Think of an upcoming good-bye in your life. Describe how you would like it to go and what might get in the way of doing what you want.

10. A therapist and a client have worked together for six months. During that time, the client's depression has greatly reduced and his life has become much more satisfying. Describe how their termination of therapy (good-bye) could go and how the termination process might benefit the client.

11. If you have had the experience of termination of therapy (as therapist or client), describe a termination.

12. If you have experienced or studied the therapy process:

    a) Summarize what you have learned about termination.

    b) Describe how this exploration has affected your understanding of the process and potential of termination.

13. If you were a therapist working with a client and were to get the feeling that the client was thinking about terminating unilaterally, what might you say that would respectfully inform the client of the potential value of a mutual and planned good-bye?

14. If you are ending your work with this workbook, how would you like that termination to go? What do you want to do as your part of the process of saying good-bye to your personal exploration? What could you do now to help ensure that you will do what you want?

15. Engage in a discussion with your exploration partners about good-byes. Be sure to address the potential in good-byes, how well you realize that potential, and what gets in the way of that potential being realized. Also, discuss any particular considerations for termination of therapy. If this is the end of your exploration together, be sure to give full attention to saying good-bye to each other and to this experience.

PERSONAL TOPICS

17. MARRIAGE

Objective

This is an opportunity to explore your opinions, experiences, and feelings about marriage.

Introduction

Marriage is a legal and oftentimes religious arrangement. It serves an important and valued role in our society and in many cultures throughout the world. Marriage can bring love, companionship, and children into people's lives. Yet half of marriages end in divorce. This may sometimes bring a positive new start, but often brings stress and emotional pain.

It is no surprise that many clients struggle in therapy over decisions related to marriage and with the consequences thereof. Like our clients, most therapists have been influenced by marriage, our parents' and friends', if not our own. Since this influence may impact your therapeutic work, it is important to explore your opinions, experiences, and feelings about marriage.

Exploration

1. Why should people get married? In particular, where do children, love, companionship, and economics fit in?

2. **Client:** I can't divorce her. I made a commitment and I can't break it no matter how unhappy I am.

   a) Describe your personal reaction to the client's statement.

   b) How do you feel about commitments and about breaking marital commitments?

   c) How might you respond to this client?

3. **Client:** The old spark is not there any more. He's a nice guy, but I need greener pastures. I think I'm going to leave him.

   a) Describe your reaction.

   b) What issues might you explore with this client?

4. *Client:* Some more bruises...he kicked me three times last night. I made a vow in front of God, but I'm scared of him...

   a) Describe your reaction.

   b) What might you say to this client? How can you be helpful?

5. *Client:* She's a wonderful person, but she does not turn me on. Why can't I fall in love with someone who is good for me?

   a) Describe your reaction to this client statement.

   b) What might you work on with this client?

6. a) Under what conditions is divorce justified?

   b) How might you feel about working with someone who is considering divorce?

c) How would you feel about working with a married client who is having an affair? Does the gender of the client affect your reaction?

d) How might you feel about working with someone who is living with someone out of wedlock?

e) How do you feel about same-sex marriages?

7. How do you feel about your parents' marriage regarding:

a) Good times?

b) Mutual respect and equality?

c) Conflict resolution?

d) Parenting?

8. Describe any influence of your parents' marriage on you.

9. Describe any ways you wish your parents' marriage had been different.

10. a) Describe the personal characteristics you feel are important in selecting a marriage partner.

    b) How do those personal characteristics compare with those of either of your parents?

11. Many marriages end in divorce.

    a) What, in your opinion, are the primary contributors to divorce?

b) What can individuals do to contribute to the health of their marriage?

12. Describe any influence this exploration has had on your view of marriage including your own.

13. In light of this exploration, describe any aspects of marriage that would be a struggle for you to work with in therapy.

14. Engage in a group discussion about marriage. Be sure to address:

- Your view of marriage, divorce, affairs, living together out of wedlock, and same-sex marriage.

- How your parents' marriage has affected your view of relationships, including marriage.

- Any projected problem areas for you in therapy work related to marriage.

18. FAMILY

Objective

This is an opportunity to explore your family, its impact on you, and how your family experiences might affect your work as a therapist.

Introduction

For many of us family has been and continues to be important in our lives. Our experience begins with our family of origin. As we grow older, our family acquires in-laws, nieces, nephews, spouses, children, and grandchildren. Sometimes friends become integrated into the family structure and become part of the extended family. There are also losses to family through death, divorce, and alienation. Whatever the evolution of your family, it is likely to have impacted you, affecting for example, your sense of security, your relationships, and your career path.

Exploration

1. Take a few minutes. Get in a quiet place where you will not be interrupted. Visualize yourself at a reunion of your family.

   a) Describe the scene generally. For example: Who first comes to your attention? How are people grouped? Who is talking to whom?

   b) Who is missing that you might expect to be there?

   c) Who is there that you wish were not? Explain.

   d) Who is there who is not really a family member?

e) Who are you eager to talk to? Visualize talking to them. What would you say?

f) Continue your visualization for a while. Provide any description here that you want.

g) What feelings have you been experiencing during your visualized reunion? (You may want to go back to a) through f) above and annotate feelings you were having.)

2. Does your family actually have reunions like the one you visualized? How do you feel about that?

3. Who in your family, besides your parents, have been big influences in your life? Describe their influence and what they did to have that influence.

4. Who are the nonfamily members of your extended family? What has their impact been?

5. With whom, how, and how often do you keep in touch with your family? What is the role of that contact in your life? What does it add?

6. Comment on where in-laws fit into your life.

7. Describe any particular problems posed by family members. How have those been dealt with? How have those worked out? What remains unresolved or unsaid?

8. As you are engaging in this exploration, ask yourself whether you are coming across losses that you need to mourn? Describe the loss and your feelings.

9. *Client:* I could live just fine without seeing any more of my brother.

   a) What thoughts and feelings does this comment bring up in you?

   b) How might you respond to this client?

10. *Client:* Since she moved overseas, my sister has left a hole in my life. I'm just not as complete.

    a) What is your reaction to this comment?

    b) In what direction might you go with this client?

11. a) How do you feel your experiences with family might color your work with clients?

    b) Describe any client issues that might be particularly hard for you to work with?

    c) What might you do about this?

12. Summarize your reactions to this exploration. How has it felt? What have you learned?

13. Engage in a group discussion on family, its impact, the implications of that impact for therapy, and anything that needs to be done about that.

19. CHILDREN

Objective

This is an exploration into how you think and feel about children.

Introduction

We were all children once. Many of us have or will have children who are very important to us. Some people relate comfortably and intuitively with most children while others find it difficult to connect with most children. Children will undoubtedly enter your therapy work through parent consultation, direct child contact, or indirectly as part of your clients' lives. Consequently, how you think and feel about children is likely to impact your therapy work.

Exploration

1. If you are at a party with children and adults, how are you likely to relate to the children?

2. If you are in a restaurant and there is a child crying near you, what are your thoughts, feelings, and behaviors likely to be?

3. How might you feel if you:

   a) Saw a father spank his six-year-old daughter in a supermarket?

b) Heard a single-parent mother introduce her seven-year-old son as the "little man of the house"?

c) Saw a child alone and crying in a mall?

4. How were you treated as a child by your parents:

a) When other adults were around?

b) When you were upset in public?

c) When you misbehaved...

    i) at home?

    ii) in public?

d) When you expressed joy or enthusiasm?

e) When you tried to assert an opinion different from theirs?

5. a) Who were the other children in your life when you were young (for example, cousins, siblings)? What were your relative ages?

b) What kind of relations did you have with them (for example, equal, hierarchical, peaceful, contentious)?

6. How do you feel your childhood experiences have affected your current reactions to children?

7. *Child crying:* Daddy, Janie doesn't like me any more, and she was my best friend.

Father gently: Don't worry honey. You'll have plenty of friends.

Child crying harder: Leave me alone!

a) Discuss this interaction. Why do you think the child got more upset?

b) How might you advise a parent who asked your advice about this interaction?

8. A concerned parent says, "It seems like Jimmy keeps misbehaving and misbehaving until somebody gets upset. Then he settles down. I don't understand." How might you explain Jimmy's behavior to his parent?

9. How might you respond to a client who said, "What is going on? Whenever I have my boyfriend over, my eight year old is all over the place. Sometimes he is obnoxious, sometimes he's nice, but all of the time he's the center of attention."

10. Summarize your reaction to this exploration of your reaction to children. Describe any trouble spots that might negatively affect your therapy work.

11. Engage in a group discussion about how you react to children, how that is affected by your own childhood, and how that might affect doing therapy.

20. PARENTING

Objective

You will have an opportunity to clarify your thoughts and feelings about appropriate parenting in part by exploring how you were parented and how it has affected you.

Introduction

Each of us has been parented, one way or another. The nature of that parenting has an impact on how we feel, think, and behave at all stages in our life. Parental activities such as limit setting, nurturing, punishing, rewarding, and teaching are all important and can be done in many ways. As a therapist, you may be interacting with clients about how they were parented as well as how they parent. Your own experience, point of view, and knowledge will be relevant to those interactions.

Exploration

1. a) What form did nurturing take when you were a child? Was there any nurturing that you particularly missed?

   b) How do you function as a nurturer now?

   c) What do you feel the role of nurturing should be in appropriate parenting?

2. a) Describe the rules, that is, the "do's" and "don'ts" and "no's," in your childhood.

   b) How comfortable are you with establishing rules or setting limits now?

   c) What role does appropriate limit setting play in a child's development?

3. a) How were you disciplined as a child?

   b) How do you go about getting others to do what you want now? How does that relate to the discipline you received as a child?

   c) What is your reaction to the statement, "That child needs a good spanking"?

d) What do you feel is an appropriate approach to disciplining a child?

4. One approach to parenting is built around the maxim, <u>catch a child doing good</u>.

a) Describe what this maxim means to you.

b) Describe how the maxim relates to your upbringing.

c) Describe how this maxim could fit into parenting.

d) How might you employ the maxim in your work as a therapist?

5. a) How were you taught things by your parents?

   b) How was advice given when you were a child, and how did you react?

   c) What is your teaching style now?

   d) How should advice fit into teaching?

6. One point of view is that parental consistency helps make a child's environment predictable so that the child can tell what impact his or her behavior has.

   a) Were your parents consistent? How did that affect you?

   b) How do you think parental consistency affects a child's sense of self-efficacy?

c) What is your view of the role of consistency in parenting?

7. If you have siblings,

    a) Describe any differences in how you and they were parented.

    b) How do you account for any differences?

8. Where did your parents learn to parent?

9. Summarize your current thinking about appropriate parenting.

10. Engage in a group discussion on parenting, emphasizing your questions and convictions. In particular consider:

- Your most prominent thoughts and feelings during this exploration.

- How your parents' approach has affected you.

- Any generalizations you believe about parenting.

- The roles of reinforcement, punishment, and consistency.

- What gets parents off track.

21. RELATIONSHIPS

Objective

This is an opportunity to explore interpersonal relationships including the therapy relationship.

Introduction

Interpersonal relationships are fundamental to our lives. Much of our daily pleasure and function revolves around our relationships. Many aspects of our personality evolve from our relationships, particularly with family members. When someone goes to a therapist, the presenting problem often involves relationships. Moreover, the client-therapist relationship is a key ingredient in therapy. Among the experiences we have in a relationship are giving and receiving the following:

understanding	wisdom	correction
nurturance	support	criticism
help	information	judgment
intimacy	humor	abuse
praise	advice	feedback
validation	entertainment	punishment
companionship		

Exploration

1. Write down other relationship experiences that do not appear in the above list.

2. Think about your relationship with a good friend.

    a) Which of the experiences in the list above do you give and receive with that friend?

b) Are there any experiences that one of you gives, but does not receive?

c) Are there any problems or regrets related to b)? If so, why do they persist? What would it take to correct the situation?

3. Think about a relationship you would like to improve.

a) Describe the relationship.

b) What changes would you like in the relationship?

c) What prevents those changes from happening?

d) How might a third party help?

4. In our relationships we tend to give some of the experiences listed in the introduction more readily than others.

   a) What experiences do you give most readily? Who is most likely to receive these experiences from you? Why?

   b) Which do you give least readily?

c) Would you like to give any experience more or less than you do? To whom?

5. Are there any presumably positive experiences in the list that you are not comfortable receiving? Describe your discomfort.

6. Think about the relationship you have with a parent or close relative.

a) Describe the relationship.

b) Over your lifetime, how has that relationship paralleled other relationships?

7. Many of us are attracted to and yet frightened by intimacy.

   a) In your own words, describe what the word "intimacy" means.

   b) Make comments about the potential role of intimacy in relationships.

   c) Make comments about the role of intimacy in your relationships.

   d) Are there any changes you would like to make in the intimacy in your life?

8. Summarize the patterns you detect in your relationships.

9. a) Describe your current thinking about the therapist-client relationship.

   b) Which of the experiences listed in the introduction are given and received in the therapist-client relationship?

   c) How might your clients' other relationships affect your therapy relationship?

   d) What is the role of the therapist-client relationship in the change process?

10. Engage in a group discussion on relationships. Emphasize those relationship variables you see as your strengths or weaknesses. Consider including:

    • What prevents addressing relationship weaknesses.

    • Different points of view on intimacy.

    • Impact of family experiences on other relationships.

    • Role of the therapist-client relationship in the change process.

22. SEX

Objective

This is an opportunity to explore your thoughts and feelings about sex.

Introduction

Even though sex is intrinsic to life, many people have conflict and confusion about it. Consequently, sex and sexuality are frequently encountered in therapy. For example, sexual functioning may be a problem in the client's primary relationship or a client may be engaged in risky sexual behavior. Sometimes sexual attraction develops between client and therapist. This needs to be addressed carefully since any sexual contact in therapy is unethical and illegal.

Exploration

1. Describe your initial reaction when you read the title of this exploration.

2. a) Who was the first person in your life to talk to you about sex? How old were you?

   b) What do you recall about the content and impact of that conversation?

3. a) How were issues of sex and sexuality dealt with in your family?

b) How has your family experience affected your dealing with sex and sexuality?

4. *Client:* I have a six-year-old boy and a ten-year-old girl. What should I be telling them about sex?

As therapist, how might you respond to your client?

5. *Client:* I found condoms in my 16 year old's purse last night. What should I do?

How might you respond to this client?

6. What is it about rape and incest that causes so much concern?

7. What is it about sex that causes so much confusion and conflict?

8. Discuss similarities and differences between sex and intimacy.

9. a) What is your reaction to homosexuality?

   b) How do you think sexual orientation is determined?

   c) How might a client's homosexuality affect your working with him or her in therapy?

10. Discuss how you feel about each of the following and explore any problems you might have working with a client on a related issue.

   a) Premarital sex

   b) The "double standard"

   c) Abortion

d) Transvestitism

e) Sex change operations

f) Masturbation

11. a) Who in your life do you talk to about sex?

    b) What kind of sexual situations and discussions make you particularly uncomfortable? Why?

    c) Does this discomfort create a problem for you? Is there anything about this that you want to change? How might you change it?

    d) To what extent are you able to discuss mutual needs with your sexual partner?

12. What problems might you encounter talking with a client about his or her sexuality? How would your client's gender affect the problems?

13. a) Why is it that therapist-client sex is so strongly prohibited?

    b) What might you do if you found yourself feeling sexually attracted to a client?

    c) How might you handle it if a client expressed being sexually attracted to you?

    d) How might you respond if a client asked you for a hug?

14. Summarize your thoughts, feelings, reactions, and any struggles in doing this exploration.

15. Engage in a group discussion about sex. Be sure to explore areas that you feel might be difficult for you to work with in therapy.

23. EXPERIENCING FEELINGS

Objective

You have an opportunity to explore your experience of different feelings.

Introduction

Feelings motivate and direct our lives and are an important focus of therapy. For example, hurt or anger can signal us that something is to be avoided and can activate us to avoid it. Similarly, desire can draw us toward something we like.

There are at least four components of our feelings:

1. The <u>event</u> (including thoughts) that precipitates the feeling.

2. The physical sensations that are the <u>immediate experience</u> of the feelings.

3. The <u>evaluation</u> of the immediate experience including labeling, for example, "I'm angry at him."

4. The subsequent <u>behavior</u>, including, thoughts, spoken words, and actions.

Exploration

1. Think about something that arouses anger in you. Get as involved with the anger as possible. Visualize a situation if that helps.

   a) What is the immediate experience that you label as anger?

   b) What thoughts accompany the immediate experience?

c) With what behavior are you inclined to respond to those feelings? How does your behavior depend on who else is involved in your anger?

d) If you follow through with your inclination, what will the likely outcome be?

e) How do you want others around you to respond to your anger?

2. Sometimes we respond with anger to something that frightens us or hurts our feelings. Is there some other feeling that might underlie your anger?

3. Now, think of a situation that elicits fear in you. Again, get into the feeling as much as you can.

   a) What is the immediate experience that you label as fear?

   b) What additional thoughts accompany that experience?

c) With what behaviors are you inclined to respond to the fear?

d) If you respond in that way, what is the likely outcome?

e) How do you want others around you to respond to your fear?

4. It is natural to avoid what we fear and sometimes this is important for our survival. Other times our fears are exaggerated or even unnecessary, yet our avoidance does not let us learn that. To what extent does this apply to you?

5. In a similar way, get into thoughts about a situation that elicits feelings of joy.

a) What is your immediate experience?

b) What thoughts accompany the immediate experience?

c) What is your behavioral inclination in response to joy?

d) What would be the likely outcome of that behavior?

e) How do you want others to respond to your joy?

6. So far you have explored the feelings of anger, fear, and joy.

a) List all of the other feelings you can think of.

b) Which feelings do you seldom experience?

c) Choose one of the feelings you listed in a) and go through the steps as in explorations 1, 3, and 5.

7. How we respond to our feelings may have been influenced by our family of origin. Choose a particular feeling.

    a) How did your parents behave when they experienced that feeling?

    b) How did they respond to your behavior when you had that feeling?

    c) How do you think your parents' responses may have affected your behavior now when you are having that feeling?

8. Sometimes it takes time to resolve a feeling, for example, changing something you are angry about or getting something you desire. Choose a situation in your life where a feeling is resolved over time and outline what happened from your initial feeling to the resolution.

9. Some people feel uncomfortable in the presence of another person who is expressing feelings.

    a) How do you feel when someone else cries? What do you tend to do?

b) How do you feel when someone is angry? What do you tend to do?

c) How do you feel when someone else is joyful? What do you tend to do?

10. Your feelings may be an important part of your work as a therapist.

a) How might feelings elicited in you by your clients provide information that is useful for the therapy process?

b) How might the feelings you described in 9 affect your comfort and behavior in the therapy room?

11. Engage in a group discussion on the role of feelings in our lives. Possible issues include:

- The utility of feelings.

- How feelings can go bad.

- Different ways families handle feelings.

- Different ways feelings are experienced and expressed.

- Different ways of responding to feelings of others.

- How feelings might enter the therapy process.

24. EXPRESSING YOUR FEELINGS

Objective

You will have an opportunity to explore your style of expressing feelings, its origins, and its consequences.

Introduction

Your feelings are part of your internal reaction to the events in your life and are an important source of motivation and direction. Many feelings are never expressed or described to others. Each of us has a style of expressing feelings. For example, some people freely express angry feelings to the point that others are put off. Others seldom express anger and may be ignored or taken advantage of. Between these extremes are those who selectively and effectively express anger in a style that is assertive. A style of withholding the expression of feelings might result in painful feelings of isolation despite the presence of others. Unexpressed feelings can also result in "secrets" that create barriers. Therapy offers clients an opportunity to express feelings and to adjust their style of expressing them.

Exploration

1. a) What feelings do you most readily express and to whom do you tend to express them?

   b) What feelings are you hesitant to express and to whom?

   c) Describe your style of expressing feelings.

d) Describe any ways you would like to adjust your style of expressing feelings. Why would you like to change?

2. a) What styles of feeling expression did your mother and father have when you were a child?

b) How did your parents respond to your feeling expressions?

c) Describe other life experiences that you feel have influenced your style of expressing feelings.

d) Give an overall picture of how you feel that your style of expressing feelings has evolved.

3. Think of a time when you expressed feelings that you wish you had not. Visualize the event and its consequences.

a) Describe what happened.

b) Describe what you wanted to happen.

c) How does this event fit with your style of feeling expression?

d) How might you avoid situations like this in the future?

4. Think of a time when you expressed difficult feelings and were glad you did. Take the time to visualize the situation and its consequences.

a) Describe what happened.

b) What were the benefits of your expression of feelings?

c) What made it hard to say how you felt, and what made it possible for you to say it?

d) How does this event relate to your style of expressing feelings?

5. *Client:* I've never told anyone before, and I'm ashamed to admit it. I hate my sister.

Discuss the possible impact of the following responses and where the conversation might go.

a) *Therapist:* Are you sure? It's surprising that you feel so strongly.

b) *Therapist:* It sounds like that was really hard to say...

c) *Therapist:* That sounds troubling... Tell me more...

6. *Client (to therapist):* I am angry that you forgot what I told you last week.

Discuss the following therapist responses and where the conversation might go.

a) *Therapist:* I'm sorry. I must have been distracted.

b) ***Therapist:*** I'm glad you told me. Would you be willing to tell me a little more about your reaction?

c) ***Therapist:*** I hear you, but I just can't remember everything...

d) ***Therapist:*** I'm not sure you have it right. I don't think you were clear last week.

7. Discuss your thoughts about therapist expression of feelings in therapy settings. When is it appropriate for a therapist to express personal feelings? How might it be helpful?

8. In light of your exploration here:

a) Describe what you have learned about your style of expressing feelings and its consequences.

b) Describe your thoughts about what encourages and inhibits the expression of feelings.

c) Discuss the role of feelings in therapy.

9. Engage in a group discussion about expressing feelings, its place in life, what encourages/discourages it, and its role in therapy. Be sure to discuss the role of therapist expression of feelings in therapy sessions.

25. INTERPERSONAL WARMTH

Objective

You will have an opportunity to explore your thoughts, feelings, and behaviors related to interpersonal warmth and how warmth might enter the therapy process.

Introduction

Interpersonal warmth is a dimension of behavior that is related to nurturing and is often associated with caring. We differ widely in what behaviors we experience as warm. We also differ in when and how much warmth we are comfortable giving and receiving and in what meaning we attach to warmth. Client comfort and perception of caring can be important in therapy as can therapist comfort. This exploration is intended to increase your awareness of and sensitivity to warm behaviors and their impact.

Exploration

1. Think of someone who in your opinion is a warm person. Picture yourself interacting with that person.

   a) Describe what this person does that you interpret as warm.

   b) How do you respond internally to this warm behavior? Why do you think you respond that way?

   c) Describe how your behavior is affected by the person's warmth.

2. a) Describe what you think of as warm, interpersonal, verbal behaviors.

   b) Describe what you think of as warm, interpersonal, nonverbal behaviors.

3. a) Do you think of yourself as warm? Explain.

   b) Do others see you that way? Explain.

4. Reflecting on your responses above, describe any changes you would like to make in your giving and receiving warmth. How might these changes come about?

5. a) Describe the giving and receiving of warmth in your family of origin.

    b) Describe any ways that your family experience might have influenced your giving and receiving warmth.

6. Describe the relationship of each of the following to interpersonal warmth:

    a) Handshakes

    b) Hugs

    c) Tone of voice

    d) Facial expression

e) Affectionate words

f) Caring

g) Friendliness

h) Eye contact

i) What else would you include in the list? How does it relate to interpersonal warmth?

7. When might warmth be disadvantageous or even hazardous?

8. *Client:* Bad day...

   Therapist 1: Tough day, eh? Tell me about it...

   Therapist 2: Tough day, eh? Why don't you put your head back and take it easy for a couple of minutes?

   Therapist 3: Tough day, eh? Those can really be hard to deal with. Let's look at what made it so tough for you.

   Analyze each therapist response in terms of its warmth and where the session might go from there.

9. Describe how warmth can and should enter the client-therapist relationship.

10. Summarize your thoughts and feelings about this exploration of interpersonal warmth.

11. Engage in a group discussion about warmth with a particular eye on:

- How individuals differ in their perception of and response to warmth.

- The possible impact of warmth on willingness to take risks.

- Your giving and receiving of warmth.

26. SHAME

Objective

Here you can explore shame, its impact on your life, and how it might arise in therapy.

Introduction

Shame involves painful inhibiting feelings related to something we have done or something about us. It can be damaging if it causes us to hide significant parts of ourselves out of fear of judgment or ridicule. On the one hand, shame can have the useful effect of bringing people into therapy. On the other hand, it can hinder their full participation in therapy. Shame can also have the positive effect of preventing us from repeating negative acts we are ashamed of. How a therapist responds to a client's shame can have a big impact on the course of therapy.   It should be noted that guilt is a personal feeling of remorse for something done. While we sometimes feel both guilt and shame about an act, guilt and shame are not the same.

Exploration

1. *Client:* I've never told anyone before... There are times when I picture myself killing my little brother when he was a baby. It still happens...

   Therapist 1: No big deal. We all have thoughts we're ashamed of.

   Therapist 2: No kidding? That's an awful thing to think.

   Therapist 3: That must have really bothered you...hanging onto it all these years.

   a) Discuss each therapist response in terms of its likely impact.

b) How might you respond to the client's statement?

c) Discuss aspects of the therapist-client relationship that might facilitate a client sharing such feelings.

d) What might the value be of sharing something like that with a therapist?

2. **Client:** I've never owned up to anyone...for years now I've felt I was gay.

Therapist 1: Oh my!

Therapist 2: You've been carrying that for a long time. Tell me more...

Therapist 3: It sounds like you have been ashamed. But, more and more people are coming out, and the gay lifestyle is becoming accepted.

a) Discuss each therapist response in terms of its likely impact and the direction it might take the discussion.

b) What response might you give and what might your goals be?

3. Discuss what shame is from your point of view. How might shame be adaptive/maladaptive?

4. Think of something that evokes shame in you and that you have not shared with others. Stay with it for a few minutes.

   a) Describe the shame feelings you are having. In what ways are the feelings adaptive/maladaptive for you?

   b) How might the feelings change if you shared them with someone?

   c) What characteristics of a person would make it easier to share this with that person if you wanted to?

5. Now imagine that a client brought up the shameful topic you discussed in 4.

    a) How do you think you might react internally/externally?

    b) How might your reaction affect the course of therapy?

6. a) Describe something you want to do that you avoid because of shame. Is this avoidance adaptive or maladaptive for you?

    b) How did you get into this situation? Do you want to change the situation? If so, how do you want it to be different, and what would help make it different?

7. a) Describe a situation where shame was in your way and you got past it.

b) What enabled you to get past the shame?

8. a) Describe a situation where a friend or relative is ashamed of something.

b) What might you be able to do to help that person feel less ashamed?

9. Guilt involves remorse for something done. Discuss similarities and differences between guilt and shame.

10. a) Should people feel ashamed about certain things?

b) Discuss your reaction to the parent who says, "You should be ashamed of yourself..." to a child.

11. Summarize what you have learned about shame and therapeutic responses to expressions of shame in this exploration.

12. Take part in a group discussion on the nature of shame. Be sure to discuss:

- Its impact on your behavior.

- What helps in dealing with it.

- The value of sharing shameful thoughts.

- What helps someone to share shameful thoughts.

- How shame contrasts with guilt.

- How therapist shame might affect therapy.

27. MONEY

Objective

You have an opportunity to explore your thoughts, feelings, and actions related to money, and to consider how they impact your relationships, particularly, therapy relationships.

Introduction

Money enters our lives in many ways. It is used to establish the value of objects and services. It is sought for security, control, and power. It is necessary for most people in our culture to buy food and shelter. Millions of dollars are won and lost on lotteries and gambling. Frequently, people are victims of "get rich quick" scams.

Therapy costs money and the fee has to be negotiated. Money issues also can be involved in the various therapeutic issues considered. Often there is a big disparity between the financial circumstances of the therapist and the client...in either direction.

In light of the central role of money in our lives and particularly in therapy, it is important to be aware of how you view money, how others view money, and how those views can affect relationships.

Exploration

1. a) What would you regard as a realistic and comfortable professional income for you?

   b) Discuss any disparity between what you view as realistic and what you view as comfortable.

2. After you have been in your profession for five years, how much would you expect to pay for

a) a car?   b) a house?   c) office rent?

How do these amounts jibe with your expected income?

3. Describe your thoughts and feelings about the statement, "I will have plenty of money during my life."

4. If you received, today, a gift (no strings attached) of $1000, what would you do with the money? How would you go about deciding?

5. What impact do you think that winning a five-million-dollar lottery would have on your life? What would not change?

6. What is it like for you to interact with someone who has

a) a lot more money than you?

b) a lot less money than you?

7. Suppose a friend approaches you for a loan amounting to one-third of your monthly income.

   a) How would you feel? What would influence your feelings?

   b) How would you respond to your friend?

   c) Discuss any disparity between how you would feel and how you would respond.

8. If several of you go out to dinner and split the check equally, how do you feel if one person had a much more- or less-expensive meal? What would you do?

9. a) What do you remember about how money was handled by your family when you were a child?

MONEY

b) How has money been handled between you and your parents as you have grown up?

c) How have your family financial experiences affected your view of money?

10. *Client:* I've just read about an investment. They say I'll double my money in a year. I'll have to borrow some, but...

a) As therapist, what might your thoughts and feelings be?

b) How might you respond to your client?

11. *Client:* I know I make $250,000 a year, but I'm still frightened about having enough in the future.

a) As this client's therapist, what thoughts and feelings might you have?

b) What might be your goal with this client?

c) How might you respond to this client?

d) How might your thoughts and feelings interfere with being helpful to this client?

12. a) Is everyone entitled to therapy? Discuss.

b) What might you do in a situation when a client can no longer afford to pay you?

13. a) How would you feel about asking your client for a $100 fee after a session?

b) Discuss your feelings about charging for missed sessions. Does it change things if your client has a good excuse?

    c) How would it affect your therapy work if a client owed you $1000?

14. Summarize your thoughts and feelings about the role of money in your life and in therapy.

15. Engage in a group discussion on money, including how it enters relationships, how childhood influences adult behaviors, and how money can enter therapy. Notice how members of the group differ in their reactions to money.

28. POLITICS

Objective

This is an opportunity to explore your views and feelings about politics and how they might affect your interaction with clients.

Introduction

To some, "politics" is a dirty word. Others are fascinated by politics, eagerly read the newspaper, and write their representatives. Of course, for the politician, it is a job. Since politics is about influencing the decisions of government, it has relevance for all of us. As a topic of general relevance, wide interest, and passionate involvement for some, it is likely to come up directly or indirectly in therapy.

Exploration

1. a) What is your reaction to the word, "politics"?

   b) Politically, do you think of yourself as a liberal, a conservative...? With which political groups or parties do you tend to identify yourself?

   c) How was politics talked about in your home when you were young? How were differing views treated?

   d) How do your political leanings compare with those of your parents? With those of your friends?

POLITICS

2. What are your views on the following political issues?

   a) Welfare

   b) Government involvement in the politics of other countries

   c) Who pays what taxes

   d) Civil rights and affirmative action

   e) Abortion rights

   f) Immigration policies

g) Gun control

h) Gay rights

i) Health care reform

j) The United Nations

k) Give your views on another political issue that is important to you.

3. a) About which of the issues raised in 2 would it be most difficult for you to tolerate strong disagreement, for example, from a client?

b) What do you suppose makes those sensitive issues?

c) How might you deal with the disagreement?

4. How do you feel about people who are:

a) Politicians?

b) Government workers?

c) Welfare recipients?

d) Police?

e) Political activists?

f) Prosecutors?

5. a) With people in which of the groups mentioned in 4 might it be difficult for you to have an accepting therapeutic relationship?

   b) What is it about you and your background that would make it difficult to work with those persons?

6. ***Client:*** Who did you vote for in the election on Tuesday?

   Therapist: (How might you respond?)

7. Politics can be thought of as the process of distilling many (millions) of opinions down to a yes/no vote.

   a) What is your reaction to this description of politics?

   b) How would you change politics if you could?

8. Summarize:

   a) How you define politics.

   b) How you feel about the political process.

   c) How you feel political issues might affect your work as a therapist.

   d) Any realizations about your political views you have made during this exploration.

9. Engage in a group discussion about political opinions, sensitive topics, and how they affect relationships, especially the client-therapist relationship.

29. SPIRITUALITY AND RELIGION

Objective

Here you can explore your religious beliefs and spirituality and how they might affect your work as a therapist.

Introduction

Spirituality and more formal religion play different roles in different lives at different times. Some individuals see most issues in the context of their religious beliefs. Others are offended by the mention of religion. For some clients, spirituality or religious beliefs will be central issues in their therapy. For others they will be irrelevant. How you view spirituality and where it fits into your life is likely to affect your work as a therapist.

Exploration

1. a) What role does spirituality play in your life?

   b) What is your belief about God?

   c) How might it affect you when you interact with individuals whose beliefs differ greatly from your own?

2. a) How did spirituality and/or religion enter into your family life as a child? What practices did your family engage in?

 b) How has your upbringing affected your spirituality?

3. *Client:* Almighty God tells me divorce is wrong. So I am going to stay married, no matter what.

 a) What might you feel if your client said that?

 b) How might you respond?

 c) What problems might you have working with this client?

4. *Client:* I don't believe in God at all. What do you believe?

 a) What might you, as therapist, feel?

b) How might you respond?

5. Give your view on each of the following and indicate the role that religion has on your view.

a) Alcohol consumption

b) Abortion

c) Death penalty

d) Divorce

e) Premarital sex

f) Paganism

6. For which issues in 5 would it be difficult for you to work with a client with differing views?

7. When you are faced with a moral or ethical decision, how do you go about making the decision? What role is there for spiritual or religious beliefs in your decision-making process?

8. Describe what you have learned in this exploration about your responses to issues of spirituality and religion.

9. Summarize any struggles you expect in your therapy work related to religion and spirituality.

10. Engage in a group discussion on spirituality and religion and their impact on the therapy process. Be sure to address areas where you feel concerned, confused, or uncomfortable.

30. SELF-CARE

Objective

Here you are asked to explore how you take care of yourself in different life areas and the relevance of self-care to your work as a therapist.

Introduction

It is generally the responsibility of adults, clients and therapists alike, to see to their own well-being. Some areas of self-care are:

nutrition	finances	friendships
companionship	sexuality	exercise
medical	dental	entertainment
rest	assertiveness	hygiene
grooming/appearance	hobbies	

While self-care is our responsibility and is in our best interest, we often fall short of what is possible. We may not have been taught well by our parents; we may have made priority decisions involving time and money; we may have habits or addictions that we have failed to break. There can be many reasons, but the responsibility is still ours.

Self-care is particularly important for a therapist. A happy, healthy, prosperous therapist is likely to be more able to focus and be helpful to clients. Also, the therapist can be a self-care role model for the client.

Exploration

1. a) Describe how you take care of your nutrition.

   b) How would you like to change your nutrition? What gets in the way?

2. a) What needs are met/unmet by your friendships? Describe your
friendships.

b) Describe how you develop and maintain your friendships.

3. a) How would you like to change your intimate relationships?

b) What might you be doing to effect changes? What tends to get in the
way?

4. a) Is your sexuality healthy and satisfying? Discuss any desired changes.

b) What gets in the way of change?

5. a) How well do you do at making and managing money?

   b) How would you like to change your financial management? What gets in the way of this change and why?

6. a) How much exercise do you get?

   b) How do you feel about your level of exercise? Discuss any changes you would like and what gets in the way.

7. a) Do you get regular checkups and generally take care of your medical needs? How do you take care of yourself when you are sick?

   b) Discuss any changes you would like to make and what keeps you from changing.

8. a) We all need fun and rest. How do you do in this department?

   b) Are there any changes you would like to make?

9. a) Each of us needs to find effective ways of getting what we want from others. How do you do at assertiveness?

   b) Describe how you would like to adjust your assertiveness. What do you think will make that hard to do?

10. a) Hygiene and grooming...how do you do?

    b) How would you like to do?

11. What has been left out? Analyze any other areas of self-care that are important to you.

12. ***Client:*** I have been feeling listless. I have no energy in the morning and less in the evening.

    What self-care-related questions might you emphasize in your response to this client?

13. a) Are there any particular areas in which you would like to role model self-care for your client?

    b) Describe how you would do this.

    c) Are there any changes you would need to make in your own self-care in order to be an effective role model?

14. What areas of self-care do you feel would be of particular relevance to the long-term well-being and effectiveness of a therapist?

15. a) What areas of self-care do you feel best about?

    b) What areas of self-care concern you most? Articulate your concern.

16. Engage in a group discussion concerning self-care, impediments, and consequences for a therapist.

31. BOUNDARIES

Objective

You can explore boundaries in a personal and interpersonal context. In particular, you can explore how boundary issues arise in therapy.

Introduction

Boundaries, for example, fences, walls, and city limits, show where one thing ends and another begins. While people have tangible boundaries in the form of skin, they also have intangible boundaries.

Such phrases as "invasive," "intrusive," "presumptuous," "busy body," "nosey," and "in your face" can refer to violations of human boundaries. If someone asks a question that is too personal, that can be a boundary violation. If a client asks to be a therapist's friend (or vice versa), that can be experienced as being off base. Similarly, ending up at adjacent tables at a restaurant can be uncomfortable for a client and a therapist. At the extreme, having sex with a client is an illegal boundary violation.

Exploration

1. Describe your sense of what a personal boundary is. How does it depend on context?

2. Give examples of boundary violations in your life. How did you feel? How did you react? What made it a violation?

3. Describe a close acquaintance who is respectful of your boundaries. What do they do that feels respectful?

4. *Client:* I am enraged by my boss...

   Therapist: Would it be OK if we explore your rage?

   Discuss the therapist's response as it relates to respect of boundaries.

5. *Client:* No, I don't want to look at what my parents did to me.

   Therapist 1: Come on, it's important to look at your background.

   Therapist 2: I hear that you don't want to look at family now. Since I think it could be important, is it OK if I ask about it later?

   Discuss the possible impacts of the therapist responses on the client.

6. Make up a therapist-client dialogue that is respectful of boundaries and one that is less so from your point of view.

7. Visualize a client asking you for a hug. What do you feel? What might you do?

8. Visualize a client asking you for a date. What do you feel? What might you do?

9. Discuss any relationship between boundaries and confidentiality.

10. Discuss any relationship between boundaries and involuntary hospitalization.

11. *Mother:* I'm cold, put on your sweater.

   Teenager: No, I'm fine.

   Mother: Do as I say, it's cold.

   a) How does this exchange relate to boundaries?

   b) How could the mother have handled the sweater issue in a protective, yet respectful way?

12. How were boundaries handled in your family as you grew up? How do you think this has affected you as an adult?

13. Conjecture how age-appropriate respect for boundaries might impact a child's development.

14. How has your view of boundaries evolved during this exploration?

15. List other boundary issues that have not been explored here.

16. Engage in a group discussion about boundaries. Be particularly aware of the differences within the group as to what constitutes violations and what to do about them.

32. WHERE TO LOOK FOR TRUTH

Objective

You have an opportunity to explore different ways of knowing what is true.

Introduction

What, for you, is the ultimate source of truth? How do you know that something is true? Where do you turn for verification? These are questions that have challenged people for millennia.

Your clients and you will have different opinions about what is true, and your response to these differences will greatly affect the impact of your therapy. Consequently, your view of the nature of truth has relevance to your role as therapist.

Exploration

1. *Client 1:* Ethnic cleansing is intolerable. The world could not stand aside and watch. NATO's bombing of Kosovo was necessary.

   Client 2: All of those innocent lives lost! No transgression is worth killing innocent people and bringing their country to its knees. The NATO bombing of Kosovo was a disaster.

   a) Which client is right?

   b) How do you account for their differences? How would knowing each client's background help you understand their differences?

   c) How might you, as therapist, respond to each client?

2. ***Client:*** I screwed up at home again last night. See, I told you I am a bad person.

   Therapist 1: You're not a bad person. Look at all the good things you do...

   Therapist 2: It sounds like you're feeling real down on yourself.

   Therapist 3: Good person/bad person is not a useful issue; there are always data on both sides. Tell me what you'd like to change.

   a) Discuss each therapist response in terms of your reaction and the possible client reaction.

   b) How might you respond as therapist?

3. What do you think about the truth contained in each of the following?

   a) A holy book such as the Bible or the Koran

   b) Encyclopedia

   c) Internet

d) Research article

e) Your opinion

f) Your parents' opinion

g) A painting in an art museum

h) A child's finger painting on a refrigerator

4. Discuss which of the sources in 3 is best and why.

5. Who was right about how we got the way we are, Freud or Skinner?

6. a) How do you know what is important to you?

   b) How does what is important to you affect what you pay attention to?

   c) How does what you pay attention to affect what you believe is true?

7. What is the role of emotions in knowledge?

8. What does the word "epistemology" mean?

9. React to each statement:

   a) Knowledge is based on reason.

   b) Knowledge is based on experience.

   c) Knowledge is based on what works.

   d) Knowledge is personal.

10. a) Describe what the phrase, "black and white thinking," means to you.

    b) What do you see as the strengths and weaknesses of a tendency toward black and white thinking?

c) Where might synthesis fit in?

11. A philosophical point of view called constructivism proposes that each of us has a personal way of processing the data we encounter. In that sense, we construct our own reality and truth.

a) Discuss your reaction to the constructivist point of view.

b) Describe the implications of this point of view for doing therapy.

12. Summarize your reaction to this exploration. Include a discussion of anything you have learned.

13. Engage in a group discussion on truth. Be sure to include how truth is determined, how truth enters the therapy process, constructivism, black and white thinking, and usefulness versus truth.

33. WHY BE A THERAPIST?

Objective

Here you can explore your motivations for becoming a therapist, any ways these motivations might interfere with your effectiveness as a therapist, and how that interference could be minimized.

Introduction

Most therapists have several motivations for pursuing their profession. Common motivations include:

- Making a living
- Helping people
- Interest in human functioning
- Curiosity about people, themselves and others
- Problem solving
- Safe intimacy
- Interpersonal intensity
- Being taken seriously
- Feeling skillful at doing

It is natural to have such motivations, and it is quite possible that your motivations could interfere to some extent with your therapy work. Being aware of your motivations can help avoid this interference. Some therapists seek therapy for themselves, in part, as a way of protecting their therapy work from such interference.

Exploration

1. a) Which three of the listed motivations are closest to your own?

   b) What reasons could you add to the above list?

2. Describe your process of deciding to become a therapist. What things about you, your life, and your environment led you to this work?

3. Many therapists want and need to make a living.

   a) How could the therapist's desire to make money negatively impact the therapy process?

   b) How could that negative impact be reduced?

4. Many therapists are motivated by a desire to help people.

   a) How could that desire get in the way of being helpful?

   b) How could that interference be avoided?

5. Therapists are often taken quite seriously by their clients.

   a) How could the desire to be taken seriously get in the way of being effective?

b) What might underlie a desire to be taken seriously? What need might not be met?

c) How could this interference be minimized?

6. Many of us, therapist and non-therapist, desire and yet fear intimacy.

a) How could ambivalence about intimacy get in a therapist's way?

b) How could that interference be reduced?

7. Choose a reason for becoming a therapist that you have not yet explored.

a) How could that reason get in the way of therapist effectiveness?

b) How could that problem be reduced?

8. How could personal therapy contribute to the effectiveness of a therapist?

9. Based on your exploration here:

   a) What personal motivations do you feel might negatively impact your effectiveness as a therapist?

   b) If you were to undertake personal therapy, what goals could you have that might contribute to your effectiveness as a therapist?

   c) Describe your feelings about engaging in personal therapy.

10. *Client:* This is hard! Have you ever done what I'm doing?

    Discuss how you might feel as therapist and how you might react.

11. Engage in a group discussion about reasons for becoming a therapist and their possible impact. Be sure to discuss ways of minimizing negative impact.